Words that are tricky to understand are in **bold**. Find out what they mean in the glossary.

Words that are difficult to say are in *italics*. Find out how to say them at the back of the book.

WHAT IS CARCINOLOGY?

Carcinology is the study of **crustaceans** like crabs and lobsters, including how they interact with the incredible variety of **habitats** that they live in.

The scientists who study carcinology are called **CARCINOLOGISTS.**

CAN CRABS AND CRUSTACEANS SURVIVE ANYWHERE?

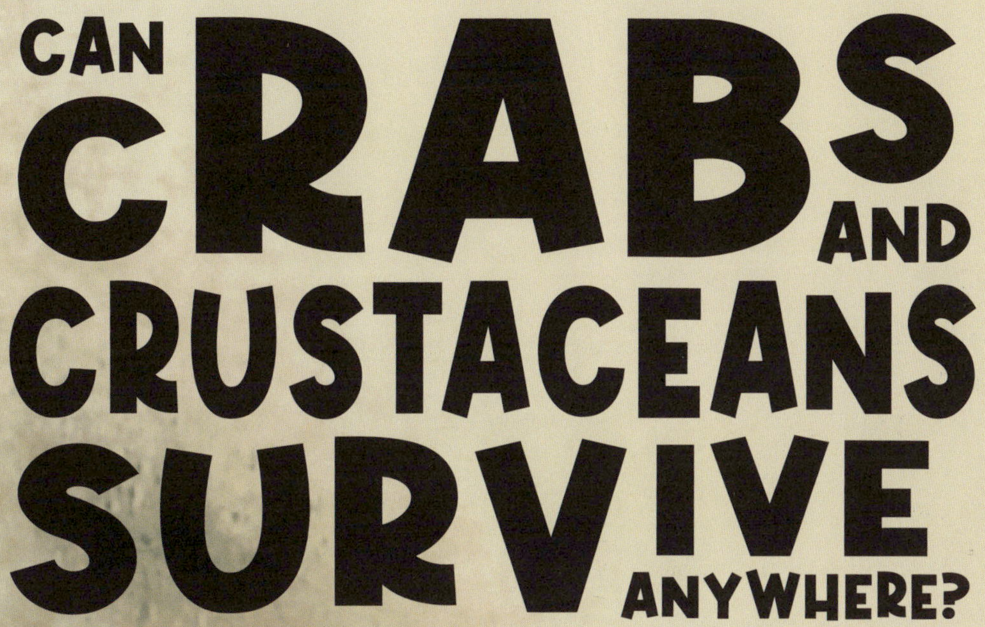

DISCOVER THE SCIENCE BEHIND **CARCINOLOGY**
(kar-suh-NOL-uh-jee)

Written by Rosie Rowntree
Illustrated by Valeria Abatzoglu

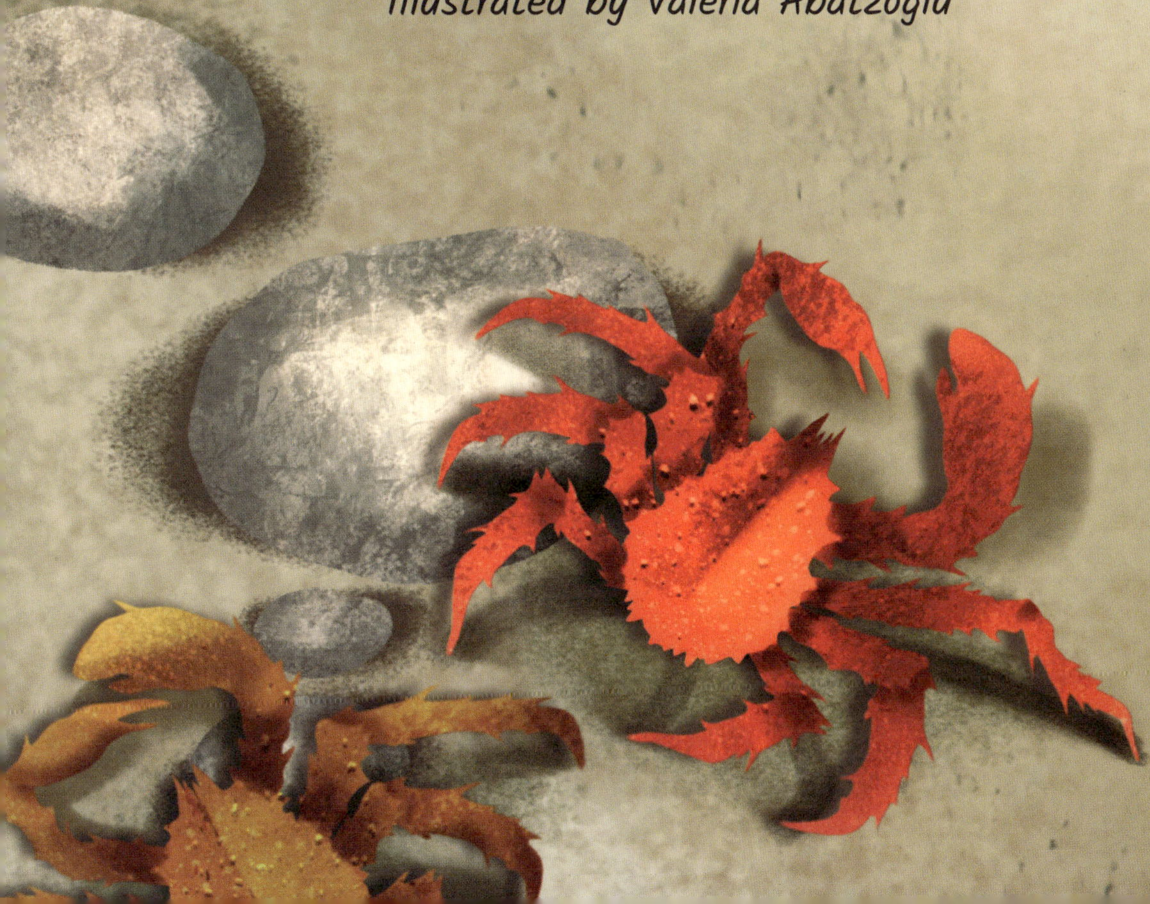

Crustaceans have been on Earth for hundreds of millions of years. They lived alongside the dinosaurs and huge marine **reptiles** like *Plesiosaurus*.

To have survived for that long, crustaceans have shown that they are very tough and able to **adapt** to the habitats that they live in. But can they survive anywhere?

Carcinologists believe there are over 50,000 different **species** of crustaceans – including many kinds of crabs, lobsters, and shrimp.

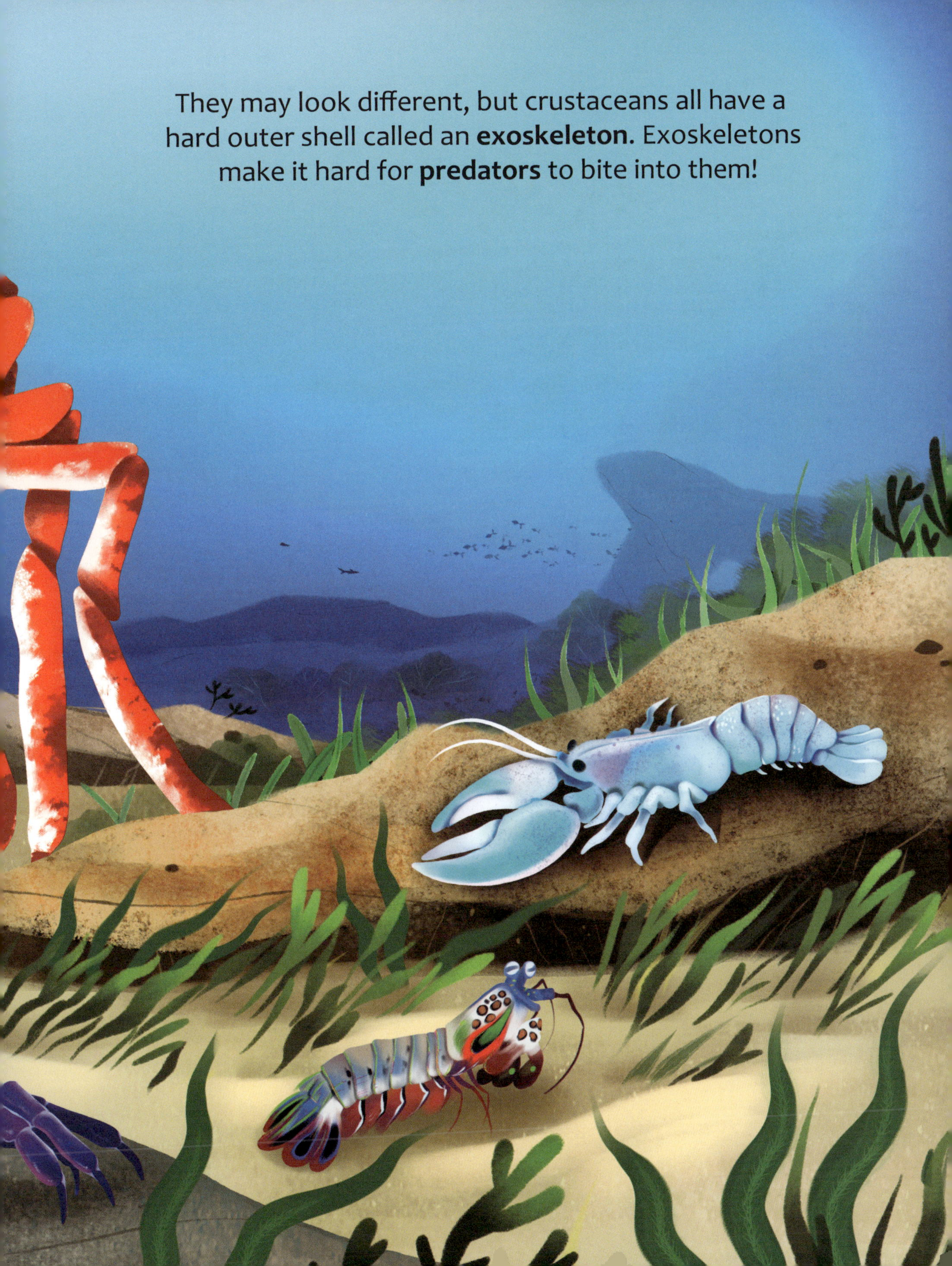

They may look different, but crustaceans all have a hard outer shell called an **exoskeleton.** Exoskeletons make it hard for **predators** to bite into them!

A crustacean's shell doesn't grow with it. When the shell becomes too small, it grows a new, larger one underneath and **sheds** the old one. This is called *moulting*.

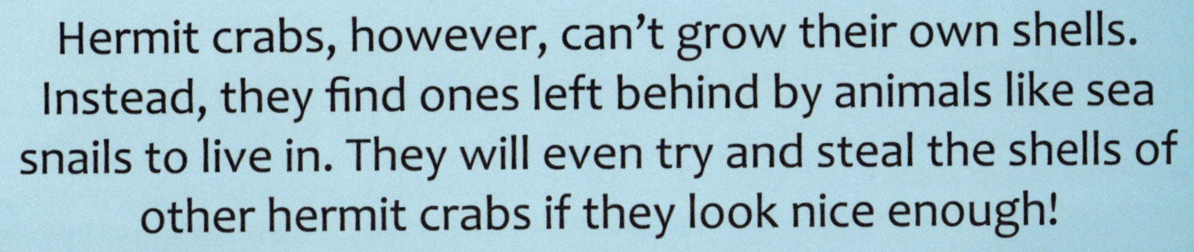

Hermit crabs, however, can't grow their own shells. Instead, they find ones left behind by animals like sea snails to live in. They will even try and steal the shells of other hermit crabs if they look nice enough!

Even though crustaceans have tough shells, certain predators will still try and eat them. Because of this, some have developed unusual ways of defending themselves.

If a *porcelain* crab is attacked, it will chop off one of its claws or legs! This distraction gives it enough time to sneak away to safety. But don't worry, porcelain crabs can **regrow their claws and legs!**

It’s not only because of predators that crustaceans have to adapt. It can also be because of the habitat that they live in!

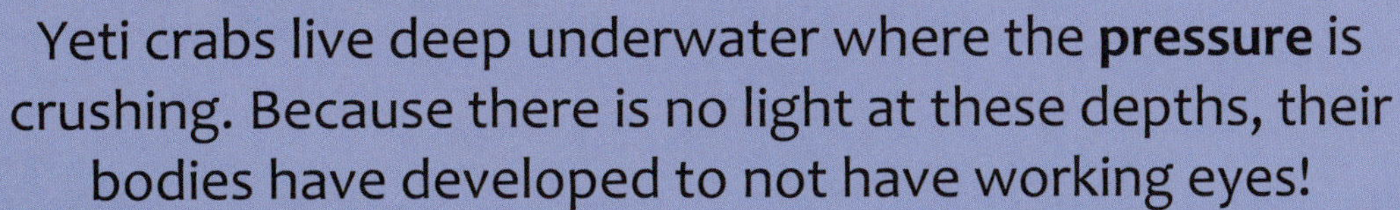

Yeti crabs live deep underwater where the **pressure** is crushing. Because there is no light at these depths, their bodies have developed to not have working eyes!

Not only that, they live next to **hydrothermal** vents that heat the water to as hot as 716 °F (380 °C). It's like another planet down there!

At the other end of the temperature scale, carcinologists have found king crabs living in the freezing cold water near Antarctica. They think there could be as many as 1.5 million crabs there!

Not all crustaceans live in such extreme temperatures. Some prefer shallower, tropical waters – like the Caribbean king crabs that live around coral reefs.

These crustaceans protect the reefs by preventing too much **algae** from growing and damaging them. With the algae kept under control, fish and other species are encouraged to move in. This keeps coral reefs healthy, busy, and full of life!

In even shallower water than coral reefs, fiddler crabs live in **mangrove forests.**

Male fiddler crabs have one huge claw that they use for fighting for **territory,** and a tiny one used for eating. They dig **burrows** into the muddy ground to hide from predators at high tide, and come out again at low tide to feed.

Some crustaceans split their time between dry land and shallow water, like the red crabs that live in rainforests on islands in the Indian Ocean.

Every **rainy season,** millions of them make their way to the beach to lay eggs.

There are even species of crustaceans
that don't go in the water at all.

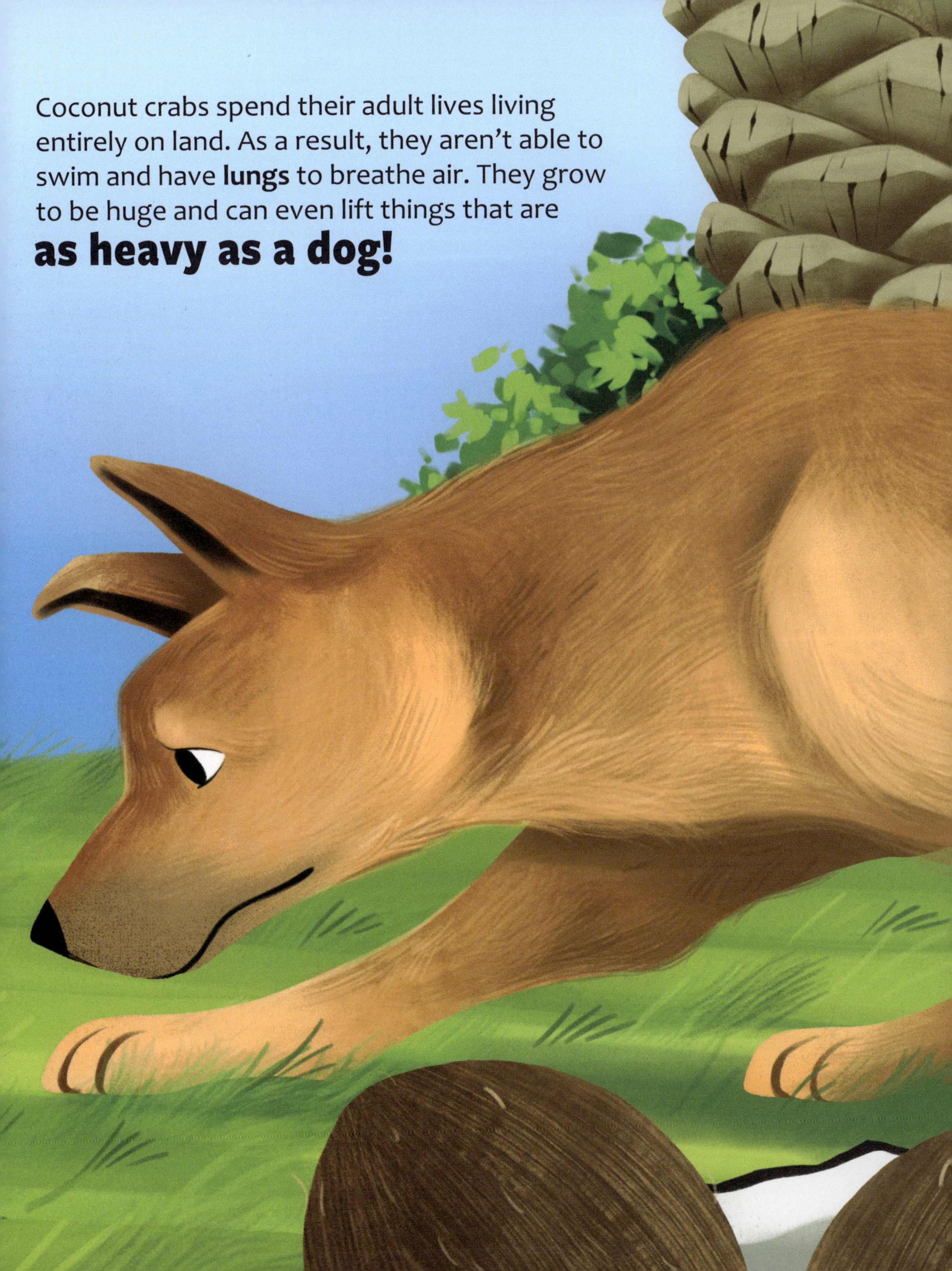

Coconut crabs spend their adult lives living entirely on land. As a result, they aren't able to swim and have **lungs** to breathe air. They grow to be huge and can even lift things that are **as heavy as a dog!**

The most unexpected place on Earth that crustaceans have been found is the **high desert**! Tadpole shrimps survive by finding small pools of water created after rainstorms to live in.

Tadpole shrimp have lived on Earth for over 200 million years. This makes them one of the **oldest animal species still living today!**

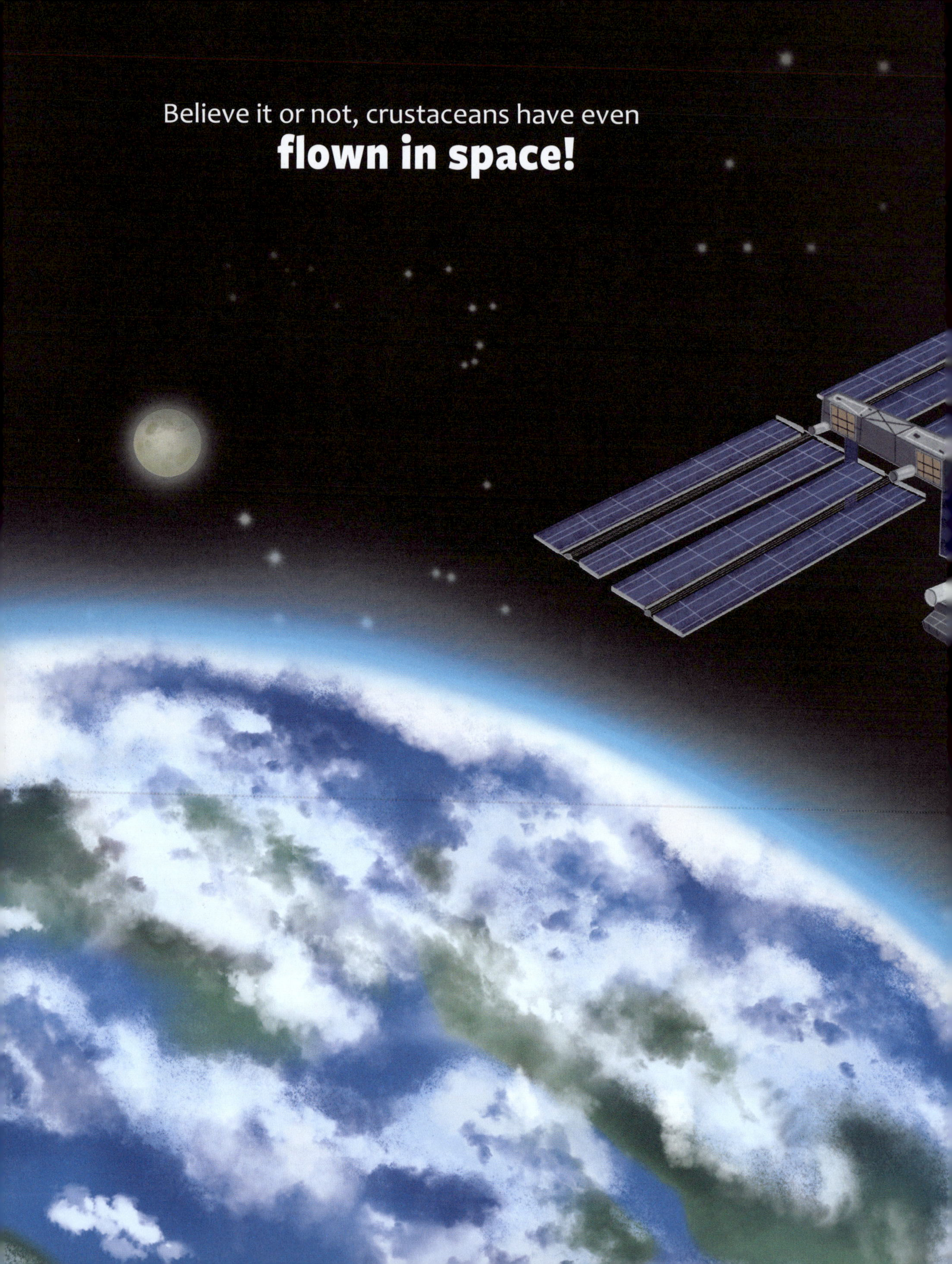

Believe it or not, crustaceans have even

flown in space!

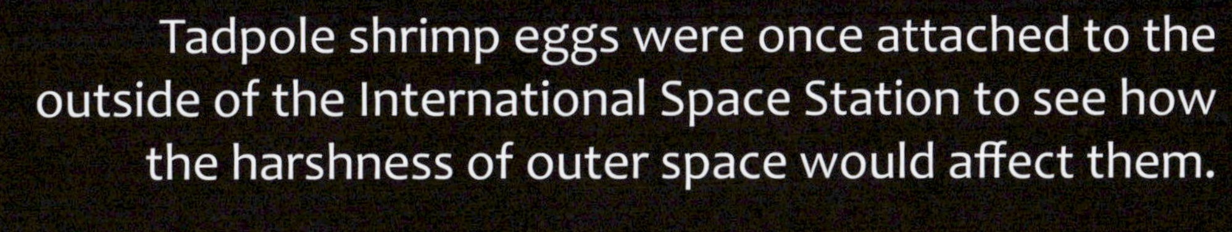

Tadpole shrimp eggs were once attached to the outside of the International Space Station to see how the harshness of outer space would affect them.

Once returned to Earth, scientists found that not all of the eggs survived. But some of them did, and they successfully hatched!

On Earth, developing a crab-like body has helped many crustaceans survive in extreme places. Some scientists even think that if there is alien life in outer space, it might look like a crab too!

Crabs and other crustaceans are amazing survivors. They have existed for millions of years in all kinds of habitats – and will continue to thrive for millions more.

Curious

CRUSTACEANS

Scientists have discovered lots of amazing species of crustaceans, from the very big to the very small. Here's just a few amazing facts about them!

TINY WATER FLEA

Ranked among the very smallest crustaceans, water fleas are no more than 0.2 inches (5 mm) long. They get their name from their style of swimming, which looks similar to how a flea moves.

GIGANTIC JAPANESE SPIDER CRAB

The Japanese spider crab is the world's largest crustacean. From the tip of one claw to the other, they can be up to 13 feet (4 m) wide!

SUPER HEAVY AMERICAN LOBSTER

In 1977, an American lobster was caught that weighed an incredible 44 lbs (20 kg). This made it the heaviest crustacean ever recorded!

SPEEDY GHOST CRAB

This crustacean is the fastest in the world that lives on land. It is so quick for its size that it can run 100 times its body length in just one second!

TONS OF KRILL

A **swarm** of krill set the record for the biggest single group of crustaceans ever recorded. Scientists think the swarm weighed 11 million US tons (9.9 billion kg)!

Captivating

CRUSTACEAN FACTS

There's so much to discover about the world of carcinology. Did you know these incredible facts about crabs and crustaceans?

WHAT DO CRABS EAT?

Most crabs are **omnivores**. They feast on a diet of small animals like seaworms and shrimp, as well as things like algae and **fungi**.

WHY DO MOST CRABS WALK SIDEWAYS?

A crab's legs are attached to the side of its body, with its **joints** facing outward. So, while some crabs can walk forward, for most it is quicker and easier to walk sideways.

WHAT ARE FALSE CRABS?

They are crustaceans that look like crabs, but actually aren't! This group includes hermit crabs and porcelain crabs. While "true crabs" have four pairs of walking legs, false crabs only have three.

WHAT IS A ROBBER CRAB?

It's another name for the coconut crab. These giant crustaceans like to steal things from people camping nearby, including pots, pans, and even shoes!

HOW LONG DO CRABS LIVE FOR?

It varies from species to species. Some, like the blue crab, live for three to four years. Others, like the Japanese spider crab, can live for over 100 years!

GLOSSARY

Adapt – when a living thing develops special features or skills to help it survive in its environment.

Algae – a group of plant-like organisms that mostly grow in water.

Burrows – holes or tunnels dug by small animals to live in.

Crustaceans – a group of animals with hard outer shells that mostly live in water. *Need help saying this? Look below!*

Exoskeleton – a hard outer layer that covers the bodies of certain animals.

Fungi – a group of living things, including mushrooms and yeasts, that are neither plants nor animals.

Habitats – the places where animals and plants live.

High desert – areas of Earth that are very dry and can be found at high altitudes.

Hydrothermal – hot water that has been heated underground.

Joints – a point in a human or animal's body where two bones meet.

Lungs – the body part that lets animals and humans breathe air.

Mangrove forests – large groups of mangrove trees and shrubs that grow along tropical coastlines. They are covered in water at high tide but exposed to the air at low tide.

Omnivores – animals that eat both plants and animals.

Predators – animals that hunt other animals for food.

Pressure – the force of something pressing down, or against, something else.

Rainy season – a time of the year with significantly more rainfall.

Reptiles – a group of cold-blooded animals, including snakes, lizards, and dinosaurs.

Sheds – to get rid of.

Species – a group of living things that share characteristics and features, and can have babies together. For example, porcelain crabs and hermit crabs are different species.

Swarm – a group of animals.

Territory – an area of land that an animal will defend against other animals of the same species (see above).

HOW DO I SAY?

Carcinologists
kar-suh-NOL-uh-jists

Carcinology
kar-suh-NOL-uh-jee

Crustaceans
kruh-STAY-shuns

Moulting
MOL-ting

Plesiosaurus
pleh-see-oh-SORE-us

Porcelain
PAW-suh-lin

THE BIG QUESTIONS ANSWERED

This is more than just a series of books; it is a complete resource. Accompanying each book is a variety of FREE material to engage curious kids with science.

www.thebigquestionsanswered.com

Use the QR code to visit the website, download free resources, and discover other books in the series.

On the website, find out incredible things about carcinologists, including what they do, some of their greatest discoveries, and the people who have made a difference in this field of science.

The material is also available for home or classroom use, supporting all the information in this book.

Teachers' & Parents' Resources
With discussion prompts, questions, and extra information around key topics.

Activity Pack
Fun activities including creative writing, word searches, and more.

Audio Book
Experience this book in audio, narrated by a professional voice actor.

The Big Questions Answered is published by Beetle Books.
Beetle Books is an imprint of Hungry Tomato Ltd.

First published in 2026 by Hungry Tomato Ltd
F15, Old Bakery Studios, Blewetts Wharf, Malpas Road,
Truro, Cornwall, TR1 1QH, UK.

ISBN 9781835691540

A CIP catalog record for this book is available from the British Library.

With thanks to:
Editors: Jenny Rowan and Holly Thornton
Designers: Meg Holbrook and Amy Harvey
The team at Beehive Illustration
Consultant: Dr Victoria Hobson

Information in this book is up to date as of the time of writing.

Printed and bound in China.

Picture Credits:
(t = top, b = bottom, m = middle, l = left, r = right)
ChWeiss 32ml; Eric Isselee 33tr; iLopezBa 34bl; Kim_Briers 34 mr; KYTan 35mr; Marek Mierzejewski 33ml; OlgaBombologna 35bl; Subtphoto.com 35tl; USJ 32br.